TRANSFORMING PROBLEMS

Into Happiness

TRANSFORMING PROBLEMS

Into Happiness

BY
LAMA ZOPA RINPOCHE

A commentary based on the text
USING SUFFERING AND HAPPINESS IN THE PATH TO ENLIGHTENMENT
by Dodrupchen Rinpoche, Jigme Tenpei Nyima

Edited by
AILSA CAMERON AND ROBINA COURTIN

WISDOM PUBLICATIONS
७ BOSTON ७

First published in booklet form as
Utilizing Happiness and Suffering in the Mahayana Path, 1988,
and *Transforming Problems* 1988, 1989.
This revised edition first published 1993.

WISDOM PUBLICATIONS
361 Newbury Street
Boston, Massachusetts 02115
© Wisdom Publications 1993 All rights reserved.

Library of Congress Cataloging-in-Publication Data
Thubten Zopa, Rinpoche, 1946–
 Transforming problems into happiness / Lama Thubten Zopa
 Rinpoch : edited by Ailsa Cameron and Robina Courtin.
  p. cm.
 Includes bibliographical references.
 ISBN 0-86171-038-X :
  1. 'Jig-med-bstan-pa'i-ñi-ma, Rdo Grub-chen III, 1865?–1926. Rdo
 Grub-bstan-pa'i-ñi-ma'i skyid sdug lam khyer bzugs so. 2. Spiritual
 life—Buddhism. I. Cameron, Ailsa. II. Courtin, Robina.
 III. Title.
 BQ5660 . T48 1992   92-14723
 294.3'4448—dc20

Cover painting: Padmapani Bodhisattva, Khara Khoto,
Central Asia, before 1227, guache on cotton,
The State Hermitage, St.Petersburg.

Cover photography: exclusively provided by
John Taylor Photography, New York City, New York.

Set in Adobe Garamond and Adobe Garamond Expert Collection.
Designed by Lisa J. Sawlit.

Printed at Princeton University Press, Lawrenceville, New Jersey,
United States of America.

CONTENTS

Sponsors' Dedication

May the merit of sponsoring this publication ensure the long lives of Lama Thubten Zopa Rinpoche, Lama Tenzin Ösel Rinpoche, and all the Sangha of the Foundation for the Preservation of the Mahayana Tradition (FPMT), and benefit all those sentient beings who have died serving others.

*The publisher offers sincere thanks to Wisdom's supporters
in Singapore who have sponsored
the publication of this book.*

Lama Zopa Rinpoche

PREFACE

In October 1987 at Mahamudra Centre in New Zealand, Lama Thubten Zopa Rinpoche gave a commentary on a short thought transformation text, *Using Suffering and Happiness in the Path to Enlightenment.*

Compiled by the Third Dodrupchen Rinpoche, Jigme Tenpei Nyima (1865–1926), a great lama of the Nyingma order of Tibetan Buddhism, *Using Suffering and Happiness* brings together advice from a variety of important Mahayana teachings, especially those of two of the greatest Indian Buddhist masters, Nagarjuna's *Ratnamala (The Precious Garland)* and Shantideva's *Bodhicaryavatara (A Guide to the Bodhisattva's Way of Life).*

The teachings known as thought transformation were brought to Tibet by the great lama Atisha in the tenth century. They became the heart practice of his followers, the renowned Kadampas, and remain today the essential meditations of all Mahayana yogis.

Thought transformation (Tibetan, *lo-jong*) is an especially powerful and effective approach to developing bodhicitta, the altruistic compassion of the bodhisattva. Bodhisattvas learn to renounce themselves completely and to cherish only others, to work only for their sake, and to lead them to the highest happiness of enlightenment.

Here in this book, Lama Zopa Rinpoche explains one aspect of thought transformation, that of transforming problems into happiness. He uses as his basis the first section of Jigme Tenpei Nyima's text, as well as the lo-jong section of Pabongka

Rinpoche's *Liberation in the Palm of Your Hand*. Rinpoche explains simply and powerfully the causes of life's problems and, since they are impossible to avoid, how to see them as beneficial and how gradually to turn them into happiness, to transform them into the path to enlightenment.

Lama Zopa Rinpoche's biography appears in the preface to *The Door to Satisfaction: The Heart Advice of a Tibetan Buddhist Master*, a more extensive thought transformation teaching given by Rinpoche in 1990. To give a brief outline here: Rinpoche was born in 1946 in the Solu Khumbu region of Nepal and recognized at the age of three as the reincarnation of the Lawudo Lama, a great meditator from that area. Rinpoche became a monk and was educated in monasteries in Nepal and Tibet.

Rinpoche escaped to India in 1959 and continued his studies in the Tibetan refugee camp of Buxa Duar in northern India. Soon after this, he started receiving teachings from Lama Thubten Yeshe, remaining with him as his heart disciple.

Rinpoche himself began teaching in 1970, giving his first meditation course to Westerners at Kopan Monastery, which the lamas had founded near Baudhanath in the Kathmandu valley. He and Lama Yeshe were invited to the West by their growing number of students and were soon traveling and teaching regularly around the world.

The lamas remained together until Lama Yeshe passed away in March 1984. Two years later, Lama Yeshe's reincarnation, Tenzin Ösel Rinpoche, born to Spanish parents, was formally recognized by His Holiness the Dalai Lama.

Lama Zopa Rinpoche is now the spiritual head of the Foundation for the Preservation of the Mahayana Tradition (FPMT), the name given by Lama Yeshe to the Dharma centers and other activities set up by the lamas' students in Asia, Europe, America, Australia, and New Zealand. There are now more than sixty such centers and activities.

Rinpoche travels constantly between these centers, teaching and guiding his thousands of disciples. He is renowned as a perfect example of the teachings he gives, displaying all the qualities of a bodhisattva in his tireless and compassionate work for others.

Transforming Problems into Happiness is a revised edition of *Transforming Problems*, originally published in 1988. For their various contributions to this book, we sincerely thank Hermes Brandt, Don Brown, Merry Colony, Roy Fraser, Roger Kunsang, Tim McNeill, Connie Miller, Kaye Miner, Nick Ribush, Ingeborg Sandberg, Sybil Schlesinger, Sarah Thresher, and Sally Walter.

Many people have already found *Transforming Problems* helpful in their lives. We hope that this revised edition will enable even more people to understand the source of their problems and to transform them into happiness.

Ailsa Cameron
Robina Courtin
Hong Kong
November 1992

1

THE PURPOSE OF LIFE

❧❧❧❧❧❧❧❧❧❧❧❧❧❧❧❧❧❧❧

*You have this precious human body in order
to serve other living beings.*

The purpose of having this precious human body is not simply to achieve happiness for yourself, but to eliminate the suffering of all other beings and bring them happiness. This is the purpose of your human life. You have this precious human body, qualified by the eight freedoms and ten richnesses, in order to serve other living beings.

What everyone wants is happiness, and what they do not want is suffering. The happiness they need is not just temporal happiness; what they really need is ultimate happiness, the peerless happiness of enlightenment. When people go shopping, for example, they buy the things that are the best, that will last the longest; in the same way, everyone wants the longest-lasting, highest happiness. According to their understanding of Dharma and of the levels of happiness that can be achieved, everyone attempts to obtain whatever in their view is the highest happiness.

The only reason anyone would not want to achieve enlightenment is that they lack Dharma wisdom. Actually, anyone who has met the Dharma and knows there are such things as liberation from the bondage of karma and delusions, and peerless happiness, the cessation of all obscurations and completion of all realizations, wants to achieve them.

So, living beings need to achieve the peerless happiness of enlightenment, and the greatest benefit you can offer them is to lead them to this state. To reach this, they have to follow the path to enlightenment, so you must reveal the path to them. In order to reveal the path to others, you must be able to see fully and exactly every single characteristic of their minds. As living beings have various characteristics and levels of intelligence, a variety of methods has to be revealed to them. Therefore, you have to know all the various methods, without the slightest mistake. Only the omniscient mind knows every single characteristic and level of intelligence of living beings and all the methods needed to subdue them.

Therefore, you must achieve enlightenment, the state of omniscient mind.

MAHAYANA THOUGHT TRANSFORMATION

In order to achieve omniscient mind, you must follow the path to omniscient mind. You must practice the entire graduated path to enlightenment, the *lam-rim,* which contains the essence of the entire Dharma, the eighty-four thousand teachings of Buddha. Because this is "the quarreling age," an extremely degenerate time on this earth when the five degenerations are exploding, there are many obstacles to practicing Dharma. Even though you may have met the Dharma, you will find it extremely difficult to continue and complete your practice, because inner and outer obstacles pour down like rain.

In order to succeed in listening to, and reflecting and meditating on the graduated path to enlightenment for the benefit and happiness of all sentient beings, you must practice Mahayana thought transformation. This means that you use whatever problems you experience to generate the realizations of the path to enlightenment within your mind. Instead of disturbing you, problems can help you to develop your mind and continue your practice of the path. Without practicing thought transformation, you cannot complete your Dharma practice, your inner mental development. This is why I thought to explain to you a short text by Dodrupchen Rinpoche, *Using Suffering and Happiness in the Path to Enlightenment.*

There are various lam-rim meditations that can be applied when you have problems. This short advice is based on *The Precious Garland* by Nagarjuna and the *Bodhicaryavatara* by Shantideva. Dodrupchen Rinpoche, Jigme Tenpei Nyima, a highly attained Nyingma lama, whose holy mind had reached very high realizations of tantra, was also learned in the teachings of Lama Tsong Khapa. This teaching does not contain anything that is not contained in such well-known texts as *The Seven-Point Mind Training* by Geshe Chekawa and *The Eight Verses* by Langri Tangpa, or in the various other teachings on thought transformation; it is just that the way Jigme Tenpei Nyima relates the practice of lam-rim to the experience of problems and obstacles is different.

With regard to this particular practice of thought transformation, there are two aspects: using suffering in the path to enlightenment and using happiness in the path to enlightenment. Here, I will be talking about how to use suffering, or problems, in the path to enlightenment.

2

Developing a Different Attitude to Problems

❧❧❧❧❧❧❧❧❧❧❧❧❧❧❧❧

*The thought of liking problems should arise naturally,
like the thought of liking ice cream
or the thought of liking music.*

In this degenerate time, human beings are especially over-whelmed by suffering, with many problems and much unhappiness. This is because their weak minds are unable to recognize as beneficial the problems and harm they experience and to see them as causes of happiness. Human beings are unable to recognize this and unable to train their minds in this recognition.

Instead of seeing all the harms caused by living beings and non-living things as sufferings, you should develop the habit of recognizing them all as supporting, beneficial conditions, the cause of your happiness. You start by trying to recognize small harms as beneficial, then gradually, as you become more accus-tomed to this, you will be able to recognize serious problems as good, even pleasurable, and necessary for your happiness. You will see everything that disturbs you as necessary. It is usual to see such conditions as harmful and undesirable, but you will be able to see them as greatly needed for your happiness.

The practice of thought transformation is not intended to stop problems but to enable you to use the problems you expe-rience to develop your mind in the graduated path to enlighten-ment. It is not that you will not receive harm from enemies and diseases, now or in the future. You will simply not be disturbed by them. These problems cannot disturb your practice of Dharma, your attainment of the realizations of the path to enlightenment. In fact, not only do they not disturb you, prob-lems actually help you to develop your mind and continue your Dharma practice.

How do problems support your Dharma practice? You have to train your mind in two thoughts. First, you must stop the thought of complete aversion to suffering, and second, you must generate the thought of being happy to experience problems. When you have accomplished this and actually feel happy rather than unhappy that you have problems, problems will no longer be obstacles to generating the path to enlightenment within your mind.

THE FAULT OF SEEING ONLY PROBLEMS

We all receive harm from living beings and from non-living things such as the elements. As long as our mind is habituated to recognizing such experiences as problems, we will only find more and more living beings and external conditions disturbing. The smallest, most insignificant matters will cause great pain in our mind, and we will become angry extremely quickly. The very root of the problem is our strongly selfish mind.

As long as you recognize everything as a problem, even being given food that is a little cold causes great discomfort in your mind. Something a little wrong with the way someone dresses or looks, something not quite according to your own idea, becomes the cause of great pain. If some person or animal makes a noise during the night and wakes you up, you become incredibly angry. The whole of the next day you complain about it: "Oh, I didn't get any sleep last night because of such-and-such." Not getting enough sleep becomes an unbelievable problem, an unbelievable suffering.

If a tiny, insignificant being, such as a flea, runs over your leg and bites you while you are sleeping or meditating, it becomes an unbelievable problem. Some Westerners spend thousands of dollars to go to Kathmandu, but after spending just one night there, they cannot stand the uncomfortable conditions and go back to the West the next day.

It is the nature of the mind to become addicted to certain ways of seeing things. By habitually seeing as a problem every tiny thing that does not accord exactly with the wishes of your self-cherishing thought, you exaggerate small things into huge problems. If you see even small sufferings as big problems and get irritated by them, you will be unceasingly overwhelmed by a heavy, unhappy mind. It then becomes extremely difficult for you to bear any problem. Everything appears as your enemy. Everything that appears to your senses will be unsatisfying; everything you hear, see, taste, smell, or touch will make you unhappy. Your mind exaggerates your problems, and your life is filled with irritation, depression, paranoia, and nervous break-downs. You are constantly overwhelmed by a completely unhappy mind, and it is very hard for you to be happy for one day, for even one hour.

You have no opportunity to experience happiness if there is nothing that you like, nothing that is satisfactory. Whatever you try, wherever you go, everything makes you unhappy.

Not realizing that this is your own fault, that your mind has become habituated to this way of thinking, you point to exter-nal things—other beings, the elements—as the source of your problems. The more you think that your problems come from outside, from living beings or non-living things, the more your anger arises. Like a fire blazing as you pour more and more oil on it, greater anger arises, and greater negative karma; unbear-ably great anger arises, and heavier negative karma. You become angry at everything that appears to your senses: the house, the people around you. This is known as "all appearances arising as the enemy."

It is said that the great yogi Milarepa keeping his right hand at his ear in the mudra of listening means that everything that exists appears to him in the form of advice, a teaching. For great yogis, instead of all appearances arising as the enemy, they actually appear as the opposite: everything appears as a friend. Instead of disturbing, everything appears as beneficial, supportive. For great yogis, everything appears as bliss, everything appears as emptiness.

SEEING THE BENEFITS OF PROBLEMS

When you have a problem, if you remember the benefits of problems and mix your problem with the practice of Mahayana thought transformation, all your problems become desirable. Instead of being bad, your problems become good and useful.

No matter how many problems you have, there is no point at all in being disturbed or irritated by them. When you meet miserable, undesirable conditions, it is extremely important to think over and over again of the great shortcomings of recognizing them as problems and of being irritated by them. There is no benefit in this. There is simply no need to see them as problems.

There are certain situations that you can manage and others that you just have to endure. For example, no matter how upset you are that your house is not gold, you have no power to turn the bricks into gold. And no matter how upset you are that the sky is not the earth, you cannot turn the sky into the earth. There is no point in caring about such things. No matter how much you worry about a problem or are irritated by every single tiny thing about a person, there is just no point in caring.

As Shantideva explains in the *Bodhicaryavatara,* if a problem can be solved, there is not much point in being upset about it. There is no reason to be angry, no reason to be depressed. And if the problem is something that cannot be changed, there is also no point in being unhappy, in disliking it. No matter what happens, there is no point in being angry or depressed.

No matter what happens, always think: "This is a favorable, beneficial condition." For example, when someone is bitten by a poisonous snake, cutting away the flesh around the bite is regarded as beneficial, although it is painful. It is not considered harmful, but beneficial, as it protects one's life. According to the

Tibetan system of medicine, when a disease contaminating the inside of your body shows some sign of coming out, it generally means that you are getting better. Coming out of the body—instead of staying inside, getting larger and larger, and lasting a long time—is regarded as a good thing. It is a sickness, but it is still regarded as good.

Recognizing as problems the harms you receive from living beings and non-living things has great shortcomings. Think over and over again of all the problems you have experienced in your life and of the result of seeing them as problems. Then generate a very strong motivation and make the determination: "From now on, no matter what problems I have to face, I am not going to become irritated by them. I won't recognize any problems I experience as problems. I'll regard them as positive." Having this brave, determined attitude is extremely important.

With this strong motivation, try to train your mind until you become like an experienced horseman. Even though his mind may be distracted, he is able to manage the horse effortlessly, no matter what it does, without falling off or endangering his life. He is able to cope because his body responds naturally to the way the horse runs. Similarly, whenever you meet miserable conditions or obstacles, you should immediately and effortlessly recognize them as good. The thought of liking the problem should arise naturally, like the thought of liking ice cream or the thought of liking music. When a person who likes music very much hears music, the thought of liking it arises naturally, without any need to consider the reasons.

When you meet undesirable conditions, if you automatically recognize them as good, you will be happy. Even during times of criticism, poverty, difficulties, failure, sickness, or even death, nothing will disturb your mind. You will be constantly happy. Effortlessly, naturally, you will be aware of the benefits of problems. And the more you see the benefits, the happier you will be to experience difficulties in your life.

By training your mind and becoming habituated to not see-ing problems as problems, even great problems of the mind and body become so easy to bear that you will have no difficulty when you experience them. Problems become enjoyable, as light and soft as cotton.

SEEING PROBLEMS AS JOYFUL

It is very important to be well prepared before you actually meet miserable conditions, since it is extremely difficult to mix them immediately with virtue. Having trained beforehand, when a serious problem comes you can easily apply the lam-rim meditations or thought transformation practices that you are familiar with.

To transform problems into happiness, it is not sufficient sim-ply to see that problems help your practice of virtue. This alone is not enough. You must clearly recognize that your problems are actually necessary conditions for your practice of virtue, and you should derive continual, stable happiness from this.

During difficult times, think that your problems are benefit-ing you immensely by allowing you to accomplish temporal happiness as well as the happiness of future lives, liberation, and the ultimate happiness of enlightenment. Even though your problems may be very heavy and difficult to bear, they are the most joyful things to have because they are going to benefit you continuously.

Stopping the thought of disliking problems and generating the thought of liking them make the mind happy. In this way, you are able to continue your practice without depression or discouragement. Thinking like this again and again, train your mind; transform your mind into happiness.

Then, because of your strong belief that experiencing prob-lems is joyful, even though you may have a problem, it will be invisible to your senses. It will not disturb your mind, so you will easily be able to bear it. This is how you can overwhelm disease and other problems in your life, such as external enemies or spirits that you believe are disturbing your happiness or your Dharma practice. You will be able to overwhelm all these. Even though they continue what they are doing, they will not be able to interfere and so cannot harm your mind.

As long as you see something as a problem and allow it to irritate you, you make that problem disturb your mind. While this is happening, you cannot transform that suffering into the Mahayana path. When you are able to use suffering in the Mahayana path, problems enable you to increase your good karma, and they become the cause of happiness. However, this has to come from your own experience.

Of course, you cannot suddenly face big problems and transform them into the Mahayana path. According to your capacity, train your mind to transform small sufferings; then, when you experience big problems or great disasters—even the most fearful thing, death—you will be able to mix them with virtue and use them in the Mahayana path.

In short, train your mind to see the beauty in all problems. In order for problems to appear desirable to you, you have to stop looking at their shortcomings. Put all your effort into looking at the good aspects and benefits of problems. Whether a life situation is wonderful or not depends on the way your mind perceives and interprets it. You can choose to label an experience "wonderful" or "a problem." It depends completely upon your mind, upon your interpretation.

Your experiences will definitely change as you change the way you think. When I was in Lawudo Cave many years ago, just before I taught the Sixth Kopan Meditation Course, I found a text called *Opening the Door of Dharma: The Initial Stage of Training the Mind in the Graduated Path to Enlightenment.* This was the only general text I found there, among the many other handwritten manuscripts of Nyingma initiations and deity practices.

I must have read a lot in that text on the shortcomings of the evil thought of the eight worldly dharmas. After that, when the local people brought me offerings—for example, a plate filled with corn and rice with some money on top, which according to their custom is called a mandala—I was very fearful because I realized the dangers of those offerings; I was afraid of receiving a reputation and becoming famous. There was much fear in my heart. At that time I was trying to practice Dharma—now I have completely sunk into the quagmire of worldly concern!

3

HAPPINESS AND SUFFERING ARE CREATED BY YOUR MIND

ↂↈↂↂↈↂↂↈↂↂↈↂↂↈↂↂↈↂ

*Happiness and suffering are dependent
upon your mind, upon your interpretation.
They do not come from outside, from others.
All of your happiness and all of your suffering
are created by you, by your own mind.*

As mentioned in the teachings, "all of existence depends on the tip of a wish." All happiness and all suffering depend on the wish. The heaviest suffering of the hell realms and the highest happiness of the state of omniscient mind come from your own mind.

Apart from some exceptional actions (those done in relation to Buddha, Dharma, and Sangha), all actions of body, speech, and mind done with worldly concern, the wish for the happiness of only this life, are non-virtuous and result only in suffering.

All actions of body, speech, and mind done with the wish seeking happiness beyond this life, seeking the happiness of future lives, are virtuous and the cause of happiness. Through these actions, one is able to experience happiness in future lives. All actions of body, speech, and mind done with the wish to achieve liberation from the bondage of karma and disturbing thoughts are virtuous and the cause of liberation. And all actions of body, speech, and mind done with the wish to achieve enlightenment for the sake of all beings are not only virtuous but the cause of enlightenment. With this attitude, not only do you perform positive actions all day and night, but all these actions become the cause to achieve the peerless happiness of the state of omniscient mind.

This is why the teachings of Buddha say that all of existence depends on the tip of a wish. Everything depends completely on the mind. Temporal and even ultimate happiness depend completely on your wish, on your own mind. Different results come from different types of wishes. All suffering comes from the wish seeking the happiness of only this life, samsaric happiness, which cannot be found. From the wish to achieve liberation comes liberation. From the wish to achieve omniscient mind comes omniscient mind. This is how samsaric suffering and ultimate happiness come completely from your own wish, from your own mind.

If you check your life, you will see from your own experience that happiness and suffering are dependent upon your mind, upon your interpretation. They do not come from outside, from others. All of your happiness and all of your suffering are created by you, by your own mind.

Suffering and happiness completely depend on your own mind. For example, you can experience suffering by following anger or experience happiness by practicing loving kindness, compassion, and patience. Your suffering and happiness are the result of how you take care of your own mind in your everyday life. It is very clear that suffering and happiness are not created by other living beings or by a being such as God or Buddha. You are the creator of your own happiness and suffering.

HAPPINESS AND SUFFERING ARE MANIFESTATIONS OF EMPTINESS

By recognizing the benefits of sufferings, you label them as good. They then appear to be good, and this makes you happy. This happiness depends upon your understanding the benefits of problems and your labeling the situation as good. You then think: "This is not a problem. I am not suffering, I am happy." This happiness comes entirely from your own mind—there is not the slightest happiness existing from its own side. The happiness that appears to exist from its own side is empty; it exists in dependence upon the nature of the feeling and the thought that labels it. So, happiness is a manifestation of emptiness.

It is the same with suffering. When you do not think of the benefits of problems but recognize them only as interferences, you regard them as real problems. On that particular feeling you label, "This is a problem." What you have labeled on that feeling then appears to you. You have called it a problem, so it appears to you as a problem. Since the problem is merely imputed to that particular feeling by your thought, even though the problem appears to exist from its own side, it is completely empty. You can see now how suffering is also a manifestation of emptiness.

When you look at or think of your "I," your "self," it appears to exist from its own side; you impute true existence to the I, the aggregates. Without the aggregates, the base to which the I is imputed, even if there is a thought that labels "I," the I does not exist. And without the thought that labels "I" on the aggregates, even if the aggregates, the base on which the I is to be labeled, are there, the I does not exist.

You can see that thought simply imputes I to the mere appearance of the aggregates. And to the different activities performed by the aggregates, thought merely imputes "I am sitting," "I am listening to teachings," "I am meditating." Your mind merely imputes "I" to the aggregates performing the various activities of sitting, listening, and meditating. In reality, the I that exists and does all these actions is merely imputed by thought to the aggregates—nothing more than this. The way the I exists is nothing in the slightest more than this. In reality, the I is only what is merely imputed to the base, the aggregates, by thought.

However, even though the I is merely labeled by thought, it appears to have an existence from its own side. This I that appears to exist from its own side, to exist as more than what is merely imputed to the base by thought, is completely empty. The I is merely labeled. Even though it appears to exist from its own side, this appearance is completely empty. It is a complete hallucination. Not even the slightest atom of this true existence exists on the I, which is merely imputed to the base.

This unlabeled, independent I that exists by its own nature is actually empty. In reality, the I that exists on the aggregates, performs various activities, experiences samsara, and can achieve enlightenment through practicing Dharma is nothing more than what is merely imputed to the aggregates by thought.

Now you can see very clearly that all the other ways the I appears to exist are complete hallucinations. The I that appears in any way other than as merely labeled is the object to be refuted.

His Holiness Trijang Rinpoche, the late Junior Tutor to His Holiness the Dalai Lama, explained that superstitious thought merely imputes a label to every good or bad experience, which is simply the gathering of causes and conditions. Without choice, the mere label that you have imputed then appears to exist from its own side. In reality, nothing exists from its own side.

Whichever way you think, the conclusion is that everything is empty of existing from its own side. Therefore, there is no point at all in becoming attached or angry. You should totally abandon disturbing thoughts.

4

THE SHORTCOMINGS OF ANGER AND DESIRE

∾✤∾∾✤∾∾✤∾∾✤∾∾✤∾

The pain of anger is like burning red-hot coals in your heart.
You follow desire, and you are not satisfied.
Again you follow desire, and again you are not satisfied.
Again you try, and again you are not satisfied.

From the experiences of your everyday life you can understand that there is no mental peace when you do not control
your mind but instead follow anger. There is peace, however,
when you apply the meditations and teachings of the graduated
path to enlightenment in your daily life and control your mind
by practicing patience, loving kindness, and compassion. This is
especially true in the dangerous circumstances that cause disturbing negative thoughts to arise.

As soon as anger begins to arise, you should immediately recognize it and remember its shortcomings. Anger does not bring
the slightest benefit or happiness to you or to others. It brings
only harm, making your mind unhappy and more and more
vicious. Also, allowing yourself to be controlled by anger leaves
an imprint on your mind, so that the next time you meet similar conditions, anger arises again. If you don't practice the graduated path in these dangerous circumstances, each time you get
angry, you leave imprints on your mental continuum that are
the preparation for more and more anger to arise in the future.

Anger obscures your mind and makes your everyday life
unhappy. It can cause you physical harm and even endanger
your life. When you are angry, you experience danger and
unhappiness and cause fear and danger to others. You are in
danger of destroying your happiness and material possessions
and those of others; you are in great danger of harming the
minds, bodies, and even lives of others. While your anger is
strong, you can think of nothing other than to harm. You wish
to destroy immediately the object of your anger. And once this
thought has arisen, it takes only a moment to harm, even kill,

other beings. It does not take long—just a moment.

Anger causes you and others great problems from day to day in this life; and beyond this life, it continues to give harm for hundreds and hundreds of future lifetimes. By destroying merit, anger prevents the achievement of liberation and the state of omniscient mind. When the heart stops, life is cut off; like this, anger destroys merit and so cuts off the life of liberation. Without the heart, there is no life; without merit, there is no happiness, no liberation, no peerless happiness of omniscience.

Anger is extremely harmful. You don't even need to think about the harm that arises from anger in future lives; just think of the danger anger causes in this life. In this life alone, your anger continuously harms so many beings.

The antidote to anger is patience. However, the angry thought itself cannot practice patience or think of the short-comings of anger; another thought needs to remember the shortcomings of anger and practice patience. By applying the meditations and teachings of the graduated path to enlighten-ment, particularly those of Mahayana thought transformation, you practice patience. Immediately there is tranquility, relax-ation, and much happiness in your life.

The pain of anger is like burning red-hot coals in your heart. Anger transforms even a beautiful person into something ugly and terrifying. What was happy, peaceful, and beautiful com-pletely changes and becomes dark, ugly, terrifying. As soon as you apply the teachings and practice patience, however, anger stops; and as soon as it stops, even your appearance suddenly changes. You become peaceful and happy, and your warm-hearted, loving nature makes others happy as well.

FOLLOWING DESIRE

As with anger, as long as you follow desire, there is no happi-ness or relaxation in your heart. There is always something missing. If you examine your mind in everyday life, you can see that something is missing all the time. No matter how much you try to enjoy different places—living in a city or on a mountain, going to the beach or to a beautiful park; no matter how much you try to enjoy food, clothing, anything that can be obtained on this earth, there is always something missing in your heart. No matter how many friends you have or how long you enjoy their company, there is always something missing. All the time there is something missing in your heart. You are never really happy.

Even when there is excitement in your life, if you carefully examine the nature of your mind, you will find there is still something missing. You are not completely happy. Watch your mind closely; examine it well: "Is this happiness complete or not?" It is not complete. There is still something missing.

That is why Buddha taught that no matter where you live, it is a place of suffering; no matter what enjoyment you have, it is the enjoyment of suffering; no matter what friend you accompany, it is the friend of suffering.

As long as you follow desire, there is no satisfaction. Following desire is meant to bring satisfaction but always results in dissatisfaction. Although the aim is to gain satisfaction, because following desire is a wrong means, the result is only dissatisfaction. You follow desire, and you are not satisfied. Again you follow desire, and again you are not satisfied. Again you try, and again you are not satisfied.

It is like the life story of Elvis Presley. I learnt about his life when I was in Melbourne recently. While eating lunch one day, we watched the life story of Elvis Presley on TV. It was very interesting. His whole life story was a very effective lam-rim teaching. In both his early and later life he enjoyed pleasure and excitement. Then, in his final year, when he felt he was soon going to die, he became deeply depressed. The words of his last song were: "I tried and I tried, but I can't get no satisfaction." During his last concert, he was singing with tears streaming from his eyes, and the thousands of fans who were watching him and listening to his song were also crying. That was his last performance.

If you examine the nature of your mind while you are following desire, there is always something missing. Actually, following desire in itself is suffering, in itself is a problem. The whole thing is suffering in nature. No matter how much you follow desire, you do not gain satisfaction. The only result you receive is dissatisfaction. This is the biggest suffering of samsara.

What causes problems and obstacles in life? What causes the many internal and external obstacles to your spiritual practice? What makes you unable to succeed in your Dharma practice? Following desire and not finding satisfaction. When you listen to the news on the radio, read newspapers, or watch TV, you can see that the many disasters in people's lives come from following desire and not finding satisfaction.

If you examine the nature of your mind, analyzing and questioning yourself, you find that as long as you follow desire, there is no real happiness. Something big is missing. Your life is empty.

In reality, both having an object of desire and not having it are suffering in nature. Having the object is suffering; not having it is suffering. As long as you do not analyze your mind, obtaining an object of desire seems to stop a problem, that of not having that particular object of desire. That problem has stopped, but other problems start by having the object.

The previous problem of not having an object of desire is stopped by obtaining the object. We then impute "pleasure" on the change of feeling that arises when one of the six senses comes into contact with the object of desire. With continuation of the contact between the sense and the object, however, sooner or later the pleasurable feeling becomes the suffering of suffering and is seen as an unbearable problem.

Until you recognize and label the feeling as an unbearable problem, until you recognize it as the suffering of suffering, you impute "pleasure" on the experience. As you have called it "pleasure," the feeling appears as pleasure—even as pleasure existing from its own side. In other words, although the feeling is only labeled "pleasure," the pleasure appears to exist from its own side.

Now, it is only a question of time before continuation of the contact between the sense and the object compounds that feeling of "pleasure" and you become aware that it is unbearable. Your mind continues to impute "pleasure" to that feeling, until eventually you recognize that it is actually unbearable discomfort, the suffering of suffering. In reality, it is only suffering.

Whenever these samsaric aggregates, which are caused by karma and delusions, meet an object, three types of feeling are experienced. There is a suffering feeling, which is normally seen as a problem. Second, there is a pleasant feeling, which when not properly analyzed appears to be pleasure, but when correctly analyzed is seen to be only suffering. And finally, there is an indifferent feeling, neither suffering nor pleasure, which is also in the nature of suffering, because the aggregates themselves are contaminated by the seeds of karma and disturbing thoughts. As long as you are not liberated from karma and disturbing thoughts, which bind you to samsara, the aggregates, you will have to experience suffering continuously, since every feeling that arises when you meet a sense object can only be in the nature of suffering.

Following desire compounds karma, leaving an imprint on your mental continuum that causes you to take a future-life samsara. Then, under the control of karma and delusions, you again experience pervasive suffering with that future-life samsara. And again you experience the suffering of suffering, as well as the suffering of change, the temporary pleasures of samsara. This is the long-term harm of following desire. As long as you follow desire, you will endlessly experience the sufferings of samsara.

The conclusion is that even the feeling that arises when you come into contact with an object of desire, which you call "pleasure," is only suffering. When you do not analyze the nature of this feeling, because of your hallucinating mind you impute "pleasure" on that feeling, which is only suffering. The suffering feeling then appears to you as pleasure, and you believe that it really is pleasure. You grasp on to that, and it appears to your hallucinating mind as pure, truly existent happiness.

This is how all your problems come completely from your own mind.

CUTTING OFF DESIRE

When you are experiencing huge mountains of problems that seem impossible to bear, if you recognize that your mistake is following desire, you will stop following desire, and immediately your mountains of problems will disappear.

For example, while you are constantly thinking of how beautiful someone's body is, you cannot stop desire. As long as you are thinking in this way, trying to stop attachment is exhausting and useless; it only causes you to develop more attachment. It is impossible to stop desire in this way.

The thought that exaggerates the beauty of a person cannot stop attachment. Only another thought that sees the nature of the body as suffering, as dirty and ugly, and as impermanent, can stop attachment.

You may feel: "I'm the only person in the world who has problems!" or "I have the biggest problems in the world!" This black view of everything is immediately stopped when you cut off desire. Recognizing that the root of all these huge problems is following desire, you can stop following desire by relying on the remedy, the teachings of the graduated path. Immediately, you experience tranquility and great satisfaction. Right then, right in that second. By seeing the shortcomings of desire, you stop your problems. You experience satisfaction and happiness in your daily life, and even liberation. Cutting off desire liberates you.

In the ceremony of taking refuge in Buddha, Dharma, and Sangha, the prayer of refuge in Dharma says: "I go for refuge to the supreme cessation of attachment." The reason the cessation of attachment is particularly mentioned rather than the cessation of anger or another disturbing thought is that all sufferings are the result of desire. If you do not renounce desire, your samsara has no end. By ceasing to follow their desire, other living beings may be liberated from samsara, but as long as you continue to follow desire, your samsara has no end.

Just as exaggerating the beauty of something cannot stop attachment, seeing as problems the harm you receive cannot stop suffering. The more you see problems as suffering, the more unbearable they will become. It is impossible to stop suffering by thinking in this way; it only makes your suffering more and more unbearable.

Instead, leave the mind in its natural state. Don't follow thoughts of "This is a problem, that is a problem." Without recognizing difficulties as problems, leave your mind in its natural state. In this way you will stop seeing miserable conditions as problems.

5

TRANSFORMING YOUR PROBLEMS
INTO THE PATH

ৎৎ৽ৎৎৎ৽ৎৎৎ৽ৎৎৎ৽ৎৎৎ৽ৎৎ

*Recognizing undesirable situations as desirable
is one of the most powerful thought-training practices.
It is the way to transform suffering into happiness.*

His Holiness Trijang Rinpoche explained that transforming miserable conditions into the path to enlightenment in such a degenerate time as this has great benefit.

In this degenerate time, there are so many obstacles to practicing Dharma that you cannot avoid them. There are certain problems, such as diseases, that we have to experience. We have no choice. At such times, you should transform the miserable conditions that are unwanted obstacles into beneficial and necessary conditions. If you cannot do this with every condition you meet, both undesirable and desirable, you are in danger of losing the Dharma.

For example, when you become wealthy, there is the danger of losing the Dharma. A thought-training teaching says:

> It is not good to be wealthy; it is better to be poor. If you are poor and experience hardships, you can accomplish the Buddhadharma. The beggar's body is the aim of the Dharma.

Many lineage lamas, such as Milarepa and so forth, achieved enlightenment by leading an ascetic life. From this verse, it may sound as if you have to become an actual beggar, but it does not mean that. The main point is to cut off worldly concern, the foundation of all the obstacles to completing Dharma practice.

Another verse follows:

> It is not good to be praised; it is better to be criticized. It is not good to have comfort; it is better to have discomfort. If you have comfort,

you exhaust the merit accumulated in past
times. Experiencing problems is the blessing of
the guru.

When you receive a good reputation or high position, again
there is danger of losing the Dharma. During the times when
your situation is what is generally regarded as desirable, as a
happy life, there is danger of losing the Dharma. Also, because
you worry about losing these desirable conditions once you
have gained them, you are in danger of losing the Dharma. And
when you meet the opposite situation and are experiencing
undesirable conditions, there is also danger of losing the
Dharma.

This makes it very difficult to practice the holy Dharma. If
you lose even the little Dharma that you attempt or pretend to
practice, your life will become extremely poor. Whether conditions are bad or good, you should be able to transform them so
that they cannot harm your Dharma practice. Problems help
you to achieve enlightenment.

When you have a problem, think: "This is the blessing of the
guru. This is purifying me by exhausting my negative karma
and by helping me to train my mind in Mahayana thought
transformation, so that I can achieve enlightenment for the sake
of all living beings. This problem is giving me an opportunity
to develop my mind."

Recognizing any harm you receive as a problem and making
your mind unhappy by thinking over and over again of how it
is a problem cannot stop your suffering. One thought interprets
your experience as a problem; only another thought that recog-
nizes and interprets your experience as happiness can stop that
suffering, unhappy mind.

Therefore, whenever a problem arises, be happy by recognizing it as beneficial, by seeing that it supports the generation of the path to enlightenment within your mind. Rejoice each time you meet an obstacle. Immediately think: "This appears to be an obstacle, but actually it is not an obstacle for me. This is actually supporting the generation of the graduated path to enlightenment within me." Enjoy it; be happy.

When you meet miserable conditions, it is extremely important to use skillful means. In other words, there is a meditation to mix with whatever suffering you experience. For one problem, apply one teaching; for another problem, apply a different teaching. When you apply the teachings in this way, all sufferings are mixed with virtue. All experiences of suffering become virtue.

Accepting problems rather than rejecting them makes a big difference to your mind, helping temporarily to stop worry and fear. On top of this, if you can mix your problems with virtue by relating them to the lam-rim teachings and using them to generate the three principal aspects of the path (renunciation of samsara, bodhicitta, and emptiness), your experience of problems will actually become Dharma. The problem itself becomes a cause of happiness. Experiencing the problem exhausts particular past negative karma, and transforming the experience into virtue results in happiness.

Think extensively and repeatedly of the great benefit you receive from suffering. Outline each skillful means. Experiencing problems in this way has similar benefits to practicing the preliminaries, such as offering mandalas and doing prostrations, or meditating on bodhicitta. It is very important to think in detail of the benefits of problems, since this is the main method of generating more and more strongly the thought of liking miserable conditions. Recognizing undesirable situations as desirable is one of the most powerful thought-training practices. It is the way to transform suffering into happiness.

Problems are just another form of teaching, giving you the clearest introduction to Dharma, to renunciation of samsara. Because problems show clearly how samsara is only in the nature of suffering, you can easily and quickly generate renunciation.

When you have a problem, think like this: "As long as I wander in samsara without freedom, under the control of karma and delusions, the suffering that I experience is not something that I do not deserve. This is the nature of samsara." When you think like this about whatever problem you experience—failure in retreat, sickness, and in particular, relationship problems—the fear and worry immediately disappear, or at least decrease. You feel less irritated and much more relaxed. Your problem does not appear as unbearable or as big. Instead of being unbearable, it becomes bearable.

Then think: "If even these ordinary sufferings of a happy migratory being seem so unbearable to me, how could I bear the sufferings of the unhappy migratory beings?" When compared to the suffering of the hell beings, who experience the heaviest sufferings of heat and cold, the sufferings of happy migratory beings are so small that they are like great pleasures. Even one spark of hell-fire is one hundred thousand times hotter than all the fires on this earth put together. "If even this small difficulty of a happy migratory being is unbearable for me, there is no doubt that I could not bear the sufferings of the lower realms." Thinking about the heaviest sufferings of the hell beings in this way is extremely beneficial.

When you have a problem, think of the sufferings that exist even among human beings. Think of the people who have more or greater problems than you. Some people not only have a disease but one that is difficult to cure or incurable, such as cancer or AIDS. Think of the people who cannot find a job; of pregnant women with nobody to take care of them; of deserted husbands and wives; of children who have problems with their parents; of people with relationship problems; of those with problems of alcohol or drug abuse. Even in one family there are so many problems. Each person has their own particular problems.

Think also of all the beings who have not met Dharma, who have no freedom at all to practice Dharma, to create the cause of happiness and abandon the cause of suffering.

When you think of other people with greater problems, your own problems seem very small and bearable—almost pleasurable. And when you compare them with the problems experienced in the lower realms, your problems seem like great pleasures. When you think in this way, you no longer dislike miserable conditions. That feeling disappears.

Then think: "This samsara is a depthless ocean of suffering." "This samsara" does not mean this place; it means these five aggregates, which are contaminated by the seed of karma and delusions. Because you have not generated within your mind the remedy, true path and true cessation of suffering, you have not eliminated the imprints left on your mental continuum by karma and delusions. Because of these imprints and because you do not practice lam-rim, attachment arises when you meet a desirable object; anger arises when you meet an undesirable object; and ignorance arises when you meet a neutral object.

These delusions arise because, first of all, you have not removed their imprints by generating the remedy; and second, you have not applied the teachings, not meditated on the graduated path, in order to control your mind. A disturbing thought arises and motivates karma, the compounding action, which then leaves an imprint on your mental continuum that causes your future-life samsara. Not only do these aggregates

43

come from karma and disturbing thoughts, but also, because of disturbing thoughts, you accumulate further negative karma. This is what causes the aggregates, this samsara, to join from one life to the next. Until you cease the karma and disturbing thoughts that tie you to samsara, these aggregates will circle continuously from life to life.

Do not point to some external samsara; point to your own aggregates: "*This* samsara is the depthless ocean of suffering." Thinking in this way, generate aversion to samsara and turn your mind towards liberation. Mix the problem you are experiencing with the graduated path to enlightenment, with the holy Dharma. Thinking that suffering is the very nature of samsara causes the thought of renunciation of samsara to develop. By renouncing samsara, mix your mind with virtue.

When you experience problems, it is also very good to think: "This is nothing. This problem is child's play." No matter what disaster you experience—even if somebody steals all your belongings: clothing, money, everything; even if you have a heart attack; even if your wife, husband, or friend leaves you— think: "This is nothing; this is child's play. I have accumulated so much negative karma in the past that, of course, I experience problems. Because I have created the cause, these problems have to happen. I have to experience the results of my negative karma; it's not something that I don't deserve. Since this is the nature of samsara, it's nothing to be depressed about. And because I have created much heavier negative karma, this problem is like a great pleasure for me. There are much heavier problems still to come."

Thinking of the heavier problems still to come makes your present problem seem smaller. This is the psychology. Actually, all the teachings of the graduated path and of Mahayana thought transformation are extremely profound psychological methods to remove completely even the cause of suffering. When practiced, the lam-rim teachings completely remove not only karma and disturbing thoughts, but even the subtle imprints of these left on your mental continuum, and lead you to the peerless happiness of enlightenment. The lam-rim is an extremely skillful Buddhist psychology, which leads sentient beings to the state of omniscient mind.

USING PROBLEMS TO TRAIN YOUR MIND IN REFUGE

You can use your problems to train your mind to take refuge, to rely upon Buddha, Dharma, and Sangha.

Think of all the sufferings you have experienced from life to life. The only refuge that doesn't betray you, that gives you perfect protection, is the Triple Gem. So think: "No matter what problems occur in my life, I'm going to rely *only* on the Triple Gem."

Not only the suffering of the lower realms but the entire true suffering of samsara come from the true cause of suffering: ignorance and disturbing thoughts. As I have already explained, disturbing thoughts motivate karma, which leaves imprints on the consciousness so that again and again you take samsaric aggregates and experience suffering. Again and again, you experience the suffering of rebirth and death. Since beginningless lives so much karma has been created, and you have not yet finished experiencing the throwing results, the aggregates thrown by karma and disturbing thoughts.

"There are uncountable throwing results that I have yet to experience—oceans of samsaric suffering. Who has the power to liberate me from all true suffering and the true cause of suffering? Only the Triple Gem. And since the Triple Gem has the power to liberate me completely from samsara, why not from these problems that I am experiencing now? Therefore, no matter how difficult my life is, I won't give up refuge in the Triple

Gem. No matter how many problems I have, I won't give up Buddha, Dharma, and Sangha." Use your problems in this way to train your mind in refuge.

USING PROBLEMS TO ELIMINATE PRIDE

Whenever you experience problems, use them to eliminate pride. As I have already explained, you have no freedom and are always under the control of karma and disturbing thoughts; and you must constantly experience the three types of suffering: pervasive compounding suffering, the suffering of change, and the suffering of suffering. Remembering this, think: "I'm going to cut off pride, the enemy that destroys multitudes of good qualities. I'm going to cut off this evil self-cherishing thought that is careless of other living beings."

When you think of your own problems, pride does not arise. As mentioned in the *Bodhicaryavatara,* being upset by suffering eliminates pride and causes compassion to arise towards others in samsara. One is also careful not to create negative karma and is inspired to like virtue.

A thought-training teaching mentions:

> It is not good to be praised; it is better to be criticized. When you are praised, great pride arises. When you are criticized, your own mistake is blown away.

In other words, one of the benefits of criticism is that it immediately destroys pride; it stops this mistake. You are then able to make progress in your life.

If you are praised, pride will arise. If you let pride arise, you will experience the result of rebirth in the evil-gone realms, where there is no freedom to practice Dharma; or in poverty; in a low caste; as a blind person; or as a slave. Even though you may have great aspirations, you will have little capability to do anything for your own happiness or for the happiness of others. You will not succeed.

The essential point is that you cannot develop your mind or your qualities if you allow pride to arise. You cannot even learn about Dharma. As the Kadampa geshes say, if you pour water on something completely round (such as a ball or a balloon), the water won't be able to stay there. In the same way, qualities cannot stay in the mind of a person filled with pride. The Kadampa geshes also explain that all the teachings of Buddha are to destroy pride.

One of the main ways to control pride is to think of your own mistakes. Thinking of your successes causes pride to arise; but when you look at your mistakes, pride disappears from your mind. For example, think of how ignorant you are, of how little you know about the extensive Dharma subjects of sutra and tantra. Think of all the stages of the path that have been revealed to you but that you have not actualized. There are subjects you may feel you know—you may know the words, but you do not have the realizations. Think of your ignorance even in terms of worldly education. You do not even understand the nature of your five aggregates and your senses. Thinking in this way helps to stop pride.

THE BENEFITS OF REJOICING

Rejoicing is another important practice that prevents pride, jealousy, or anger. Whenever you hear that somebody has been successful, rejoice. You should always practice rejoicing, even about samsaric success. For example, when you hear that someone has been successful in business, you should rejoice. When you hear that someone—whether your friend or your enemy—has found a partner, again rejoice: "How wonderful it is that they have found the happiness they were seeking!" Feel as happy for them as you do for yourself when you find something that you have been wanting. In other words, cherish others as you cherish yourself. Feel happy when others find happiness, as if you yourself had found happiness.

If you cherish only yourself, you cannot experience happiness, but if you cherish others as you cherish yourself, it arises naturally. When you cherish others, if someone finds the happiness they were seeking, you naturally feel happy, without any need to think of the reasons. When something good happens to someone, you naturally feel happy.

When you see a body-builder with a good body, think: "How wonderful it is that this person has a beautiful body now as a result of practicing patience and morality in past lives." When you see someone who is very wealthy, think: "How wonderful it is that this person is experiencing this good karma as a result of giving charity to other beings and making offerings to the Triple Gem in the past." If someone is very intelligent or has more understanding of Dharma than you, you should also rejoice. And if someone has done many retreats, even though you have not had the chance to do any, rejoice for them.

If you take all these opportunities to rejoice, you accumulate inconceivable merit. If the other person has a lower level of mind than you, by rejoicing about the merit they have accumulated, you accumulate even more merit than they do—twice as much. If the other person has a higher level of mind than you, you accumulate half as much merit by rejoicing.

Simply by rejoicing, without the need for extensive preparation or any special effort of body or speech, you can accumulate incredible merit. In one second you can accumulate merit infinite as space. If you can really do it, rejoicing is the easiest and most extensive way to accumulate merit.

Immediately rejoicing when you find good qualities in others also stops feelings of jealousy. When you feel jealous, there is a danger that you might attempt to interfere with the success and happiness of others. But if you abandon jealousy and practice rejoicing, even though you are not successful now, you create the cause to be successful in the future. By rejoicing now when others are able to do much Dharma practice and retreat and gain understanding and realizations, you create the cause to have these experiences yourself later.

Allowing pride and jealousy to arise creates only obstacles to success now and in the future—obstacles not only to practicing Dharma and developing your mind but even to success in the worldly activities of this life. Rejoicing is a skillful psychological method to prevent this and a very important part of everyday life. Rejoicing when others achieve samsaric success and find the happiness they seek solves many problems.

If you do not practice rejoicing, exchanging yourself with others, no matter how many years you have this precious human body, no matter how much wealth, intelligence, or worldly or Dharma education you have, there can be no happiness or peace in your life. It is the inability to rejoice that drives people crazy and motivates crazy actions. Then, no matter how long you live, you are crazy.

By having a perfect human body and the Buddha-potential within your heart, you can bring unbelievably extensive benefits to yourself and to other living beings. But if you do not apply these practices in your daily life, you yourself have cut off all these benefits.

Using Problems to Purify Negative Karma

Another benefit of having problems is that you can use them to purify negative karma. Think: "All my problems come only from my negative karma." Remember the four outlines of karma and apply them to your present problems: karma is definite; karma is expandable; one cannot experience a result without having created its cause; and once created, karma is never lost.

If, for example, you are experiencing disharmony in a relationship, or if you lose your partner, remember your own particular negative karma in this life; also remember that you have created negative karma in past lives: out of selfishness, you must have engaged in sexual misconduct and destroyed harmonious relationships between other people.

Think in this way: "I have created negative karma, so I will definitely experience its results. The reason I have been experiencing these problems again and again for such a long time is that karma is expandable. If I had abandoned sexual misconduct and other negative karma in past lives, I would not be experiencing these problems now. My relationship is not harmonious but is instead full of quarrels and problems because I did not abstain from sexual misconduct in past lives. If I had lived in virtue and morality in my past lives, my life now would be happy and harmonious. Because I have not created this good karma, I am not experiencing this result now."

Even though it may be one hundred eons before you experience the results, the karma you have accumulated is never lost. When the right time and perfect conditions occur, the karma ripens. So, think: "In the past, I did not purify my negative karma with the four opponent powers and did not apply the remedy, the path. This means that I haven't created any condition to stop my experiencing the results of this karma. Because I did nothing to counteract my negative karma, I am now experiencing the results." Apply the four outlines of karma to your present problem in this way.

Think well, then tell yourself: "This problem is a teaching for me. It is telling me that if I don't like this problem, I should abandon the cause, non-virtue." With regard to any negative karma already accumulated in the past, the first thing to do is to confess by applying the four opponent powers, and the second important thing is to abstain from committing the negative karma again. In this way, the problem becomes an extremely beneficial teaching.

For example, after using black magic to kill many people and animals, Milarepa felt: "I am a very evil person. I must confess and purify all this and practice Dharma." Milarepa was advised by the person who taught him black magic to go to see Marpa. With the strong wish to practice Dharma, Milarepa went to meet Marpa, and he became enlightened in that lifetime.

There are many similar stories of people who, after experiencing some heavy problem, got completely fed up with worldly life, went to find a guru, received teachings, and then did retreat in a solitary place. They practiced and achieved the three principal aspects of the path, high realizations of tantra, and finally, enlightenment. This has happened many times, to many people: lay people, monks, and nuns. In the beginning, they had no intention to dedicate their lives completely to Dharma, but then the experience of some heavy problem caused them to generate complete renunciation. Later, they became very pure Dharma practitioners, practicing despite many hardships and achieving very high realizations of the path.

Do not abstain from creating only heavy negative karma; as much as possible abandon even the smallest negative actions. You desire not only great enjoyments, but even the smallest comfort, even in your dreams. And besides not wanting big problems, you do not want even the smallest discomfort; you do not want even an unpleasant dream. Therefore, you should abandon even the smallest negative karma.

USING PROBLEMS AS AN INSPIRATION TO PRACTICE VIRTUE

Another benefit of problems is that through them you come to like virtue. "Miserable conditions persuade you to practice virtue." His Holiness Trijang Rinpoche once explained that problems warn you that if you do not like suffering, you must abandon negative actions, purify past negative karma, and attempt to accumulate merit. While you are experiencing a problem, what you actually want is happiness, which is the absence of that problem. Think: "If I want happiness, the absence of this problem, I should create the cause for it." In this way you use everyday problems as a teaching. They inspire you to create virtue, the cause of happiness.

If your life is free of problems, you become totally distracted by your comfortable life and do not remember to practice Dharma. Problems, such as being wrongly accused or suffering from disease or loss, cause you to renounce samsara and attempt to practice virtue.

Since you like to have even the smallest comfort, you should accumulate not only extensive merits but also the smallest virtue. If you have the opportunity to accumulate virtue even while doing the four types of actions (eating, walking, sitting, sleeping), you should take it. For example, every time you eat or drink, take the opportunity to create virtue by offering your food or drink to the Triple Gem. As much as you can, cherish all the beings—human and animal—around you with a good heart, and try to benefit them by giving them whatever help they need. Give them every single thing you can to make them happy: even a few sweet words or some interesting conversation that benefits their minds, that stops their problems and makes them happy. Use every opportunity, every action of your body, speech, and mind, to increase your virtue.

USING PROBLEMS TO TRAIN YOUR MIND IN COMPASSION
AND LOVING KINDNESS

Problems also give you the opportunity to train your mind in compassion. Unless they are crazy, everyone accepts this as a good thing. Even people who do not accept reincarnation or karma agree that it is very good to have compassion.

Think of the many beings who are experiencing problems similar to yours and as well as those who are experiencing more or greater problems. Even if they have the same problem, it may be a greater hardship for them, or they may be experiencing many other problems as well.

Think: "Just as I want happiness and do not want suffering, everyone else also wants happiness and does not want suffering. We are exactly the same. How good it would be if all these beings were freed from all their sufferings." On top of generating immeasurable compassion like this, generate great compassion by thinking: "*I* will free them from all their sufferings." Use your problems in this way to train your mind in great compassion.

When other people disrespect you or treat you badly, it is extremely effective to remember the following verse from the *Bodhicaryavatara:*

> My karma induced me to receive this harm. But
> didn't I harm this person by causing them to be
> lost in the pit of the hells?

Shantideva is saying that you receive harm from a particular person because in past lives you created a link with them by harming them. That karma then causes them to harm you in this life. They are obliged to create negative karma by harming you, and this negative karma causes them to fall down into the pit of the hells. By forcing them to create this negative karma, you actually throw them into the hells.

If you remember this verse when someone causes you problems, there is no possibility at all that anger will arise. Instead, compassion for them will arise naturally, without choice. Because you are motivated by compassion, you want only to help the person with your body, speech, and mind, rather than to retaliate. You want only to pacify their mind, to stop them from creating negative karma and help them to purify the negative karma they have already accumulated.

In a similar way, you can use your problems to train your mind in loving kindness. When you have a problem, you are devoid of temporal and ultimate happiness. Remember all the other beings who are also without temporal and ultimate happiness. You and they are exactly the same in wanting happiness. Think: "How wonderful it would be if all living beings had happiness." Do not generate only immeasurable loving kindness but also great loving kindness: "*I* will cause them all to have happiness."

6

EXPERIENCING YOUR PROBLEMS FOR OTHERS

୧୬୫୧୬୧୬୫୧୬୧୬୫୧୬୧୬୫୧୬୧୬୫୧୬

Experience every single undesirable thing
on behalf of all other living beings.

Problems benefit you by giving you the opportunity to train your mind in bodhicitta, so that you come to feel it is unbearable that other beings experience suffering. Practicing bodhicitta, exchanging yourself for others, means renouncing yourself rather than others and cherishing others rather than yourself.

In the *Bodhicaryavatara,* the great bodhisattva Shantideva says that unless you exchange yourself for others, you cannot become enlightened, and even in samsara there can be no happiness. Forget about future lives—you cannot succeed even in the activities of this life. No matter how much you want happiness in your everyday life, you cannot experience it unless you develop a good heart. Without a good heart, you will never have peace in your life.

The practice of bodhicitta is not only for those who seek enlightenment or the happiness of future lives; it is even for those who do not know about or do not accept reincarnation and karma. Virtue results in happiness; non-virtue in suffering. As long as they want happiness and do not want suffering, even worldly people with aims no higher than to achieve happiness in this life—and only their own happiness, not that of others—must practice the good heart, bodhicitta. This means exchanging themselves for others: renouncing themselves and cherishing others.

Even though a bodhisattva might experience problems as a result of negative karma from past lives, they experience them for the sake of other living beings. Instead of being problems, they become happiness; instead of being miserable conditions, they become happy conditions; instead of causing a miserable life, they cause a happy life. If you practice renouncing yourself and cherishing others, you can experience your problems for the sake of others. In this way, you have a happy life. Problems do not disturb you; they only help you to actualize the graduated path to enlightenment.

In order to achieve enlightenment for the sake of all living beings, you must destroy your enemy, the self-cherishing thought, the greatest enemy to your own success and that of all other living beings. As long as the self-cherishing thought is dwelling in your heart, there is no space to generate bodhicitta, so there is no way to achieve enlightenment and perfectly guide all living beings.

Following your selfish mind brings only problems, failure, and disharmony. The stronger your selfish mind is, the stronger is your anger, jealousy, attachment, and dissatisfaction. The more selfish you are, the more attachment and dissatisfaction you have, and thus the more problems you experience in your daily life, one after another.

Your selfish mind wants you to be the best. It wants you to have the best reputation and the most wealth, and others to be poorer and weaker. It wants you to be first among all others. Your selfish mind wants you to succeed and others to fail. However, when the expectations of your selfish mind are not met, jealousy, anger, ill will, strong attachment, and other disturbing thoughts arise. Under the control of these negative thoughts, you perform various unskillful actions and accumulate negative karma. Besides the fact that you do not experience even temporal happiness as a result of this negative karma, your experience in future lives will be only the suffering of suffering.

The less you practice exchanging yourself for others and the stronger your selfish mind, the more disturbing you will find living beings and non-living things. The more you cherish yourself and are concerned about your own happiness—"I have this problem, I have that problem. When will I be happy?"—the more you will experience disturbances and harm, and the more you will recognize these as problems.

Every time a problem arises, the essential thing is to be aware immediately that it comes from your selfish mind, that it is given to you by your self-cherishing thought. Every time you have a problem, you should immediately try to recognize this evolution. As long as you put all the blame outside, there can be no happiness. In reality, all the difficulties of life come from the self-cherishing thought; all problems are the result of negative karma accumulated in the past out of self-cherishing. Under the control of self-cherishing, you allowed disturbing thoughts to arise, which motivated this negative karma. The problems you experience in your life are related not only to past negative karma accumulated under the control of the self-cherishing thought, but also to the self-cherishing thought in your present daily life.

One of the most important of the five powers taught in *The Seven-Point Mind Training* is putting all the blame on the self-cherishing thought. In this way you develop aversion to the self-cherishing thought, seeing it as your enemy. Instead of becoming one with the self-cherishing thought, you separate yourself from it, and then all your daily activities become pure Dharma.

No matter what difficult circumstances arise, put all the blame on the self-cherishing thought. Think that every difficulty is the shortcoming of self-cherishing. As well as that, give back to the self-cherishing thought all the problems and undesirable things that the self-cherishing thought has given you. Use your problems as weapons to destroy self-cherishing. If you can use the problem you are experiencing to destroy the self-cherishing thought, especially if the problem is one that you cannot avoid, your experience of problems really becomes Dharma.

Experiencing problems on behalf of others, exchanging yourself for others, is the practice of bodhicitta. There is no question that this is the most skillful means of accumulating extensive merit in a very short time and is the greatest purification. Even if you cannot do this practice, however, give every undesirable thing that happens to you back to the self-cherishing thought in order to destroy it. Every problem you experience then becomes pure Dharma. Experiencing problems becomes the remedy to self-cherishing, which is the best Dharma practice. Using the difficulties in your life in this way becomes virtue. Even though a person may not rely upon Buddha, Dharma, and Sangha or have faith in the teachings on karma, if they use their problems to destroy their own selfish mind, they are practicing pure Dharma.

Put all the blame on your self-cherishing thought. Instead of thinking, "This is *my* problem," think that it is the problem of your self-cherishing thought, and then destroy the self-cherishing by giving the problem back to it. It is especially good to use your fears of bad reputation and criticism to destroy self-cherishing. In this way, fears, worries, and paranoia cannot arise. This is the deep, essential psychology that really hits the self-cherishing thought, the source of all your problems, and makes it non-existent.

There are many problems in life that you have to endure, that you have to experience again and again, or that you have to learn to live with: certain diseases, physical disability, paralysis, spirit harms, imperfect senses, having a disabled child. Some people are always being scolded or beaten by an alcoholic wife or husband. Whenever they are home, there is always quarreling and fighting. All their time together is spent quarreling. They do not separate, and there is always unhappiness and disharmony in their lives. You may be trapped in a heavy situation of this kind, with no power to change anything and no freedom to escape. The best thing to do is to think: "All these problems have been given to me by my self-cherishing thought." Give all these problems back to your self-cherishing thought. And then decide to experience your problems on behalf of others. This is the bravest, most powerful practice you can do.

Think: "The reason that I have not yet been released from these problems is that from beginningless lifetimes I have cherished myself and renounced other living beings. From now on, I'm going to live my life only with bodhicitta. I'm going to cherish others, which is the source of all happiness." If you change your attitude from cherishing yourself to cherishing others, all your problems stop. All confusion is stopped simply by changing your attitude. This one practice of exchanging yourself with others stops all the confusion and problems in life.

TAKING AND GIVING

When you have a problem, apply the Mahayana thought transformation practice of *tong-len* (taking and giving). Take all the suffering of other beings into your own heart, and give everything—your own body, possessions, happiness, and merit—to others. Since many other beings have the same problem as you, take upon yourself their experience of that particular problem, as well as the suffering and causes of suffering of all other beings. In this way, you experience your problem for others.

When you think that you are experiencing the problem for other living beings, you transform your experience of the problem into virtue. Because you are experiencing your problem on behalf of all those with similar problems, as well as other problems, your experience becomes great purification and a skillful means to accumulate extensive merit. As the number of beings for whom you experience the suffering is infinite, you accumulate infinite merit.

TRANSFORMING ILLNESS INTO THE PATH

Another thought-training teaching says: "Disease is the broom that cleans away negative karma and obscurations." You can feel happy when you become sick by thinking: "The negative karma that I've accumulated in the past, which I definitely have to experience, has ripened on this body in this life. If it had not, I would have to experience the results of that negative karma during inconceivable lifetimes in the lower realms." Thinking like this allows you to live your life with a relaxed, happy mind. You do not get depressed or upset about anything. As your mind is relaxed, external conditions do not disturb you, and you are able to continue your Dharma practice.

Also think: "In the past I have practiced tong-len, taking other beings' suffering upon myself and dedicating my body, possessions, happiness, and merits to others. Now I have received the sufferings, negative karma, and obscurations of others—so, I have succeeded. My wish has been granted." Generate happiness by thinking like this.

Pabongka Dechen Nyingpo advised that when your disease gets worse and worse, you should think: "My illness means I have succeeded in my tong-len practice. By using my problems to practice taking and giving, I have accumulated inconceivable merit, the cause of happiness, and done much purification. If I were to recover now, I would lose this opportunity to practice Dharma. I wouldn't have any chance to practice the skillful means of tong-len, which enables me to accumulate inconceivable merit and purify my obscurations. How fortunate I am that my problem has not stopped! If I didn't have this problem, I would become lazy. I would hardly practice any purification or accumulate any merit." As I mentioned before, don't think that only this particular suffering of others has ripened upon you, but that all the sufferings of other beings have ripened upon you as well. "I have received the present sufferings of all other beings and all the future sufferings they will have to experience until samsara ends. I am experiencing these on their behalf." His Holiness Trijang Rinpoche explained that we should also think: "How fantastic it is that I am actually able to take upon myself the sufferings of living beings at this time!" Rejoice and feel happy. Practicing tong-len in this way, completely renouncing yourself for others, could become like the practice of the monk-disciple of Kunpang Drag-gyen, who completely recovered from leprosy through the practice of taking and giving.

When you are doing an intensive meditation retreat on thought transformation, in the breaks between sessions you should make requests to the Guru-Triple Gem to be able to use your suffering in the Mahayana path. When your mental capacity is a little more advanced, make offerings to the Triple Gem, the protectors, and the harmful spirits, and ask to receive the sufferings and problems of other living beings upon yourself. You request the spirits to give all their harms, all undesirable things, such as disease or failure, to you rather than to others. You ask to experience all these bad conditions on behalf of other living beings.

A thought-training teaching explains:

> "Spirit possessions are transformations of the Victorious One. Suffering is a manifestation of emptiness."

When you are being harmed by spirits and are experiencing terrifying dreams in the daytime and nighttime, do not think that this is a spirit, but instead see it as a transformation of Buddha. If you meditate on the spirit as your deity, it will be unable to harm you. Thinking of spirit harms as transformations of the

Victorious One means the spirits cannot disturb your practice, so your mind is happy. This is one way to protect yourself.

Even if disturbing thoughts have arisen uncontrollably, or you have created negative karma, such as transgressing your vows or breaking your guru's advice, use thought transformation. Think: "While practicing tong-len, I have been praying to receive upon myself all the undesirable experiences of other living beings. Now my prayer has been answered. I am receiving all the undesirable experiences of others and experiencing them on their behalf."

Then pray: "May this negative karma represent the negative karma of all those who have transgressed the three levels of vows and have thus cut off the root of liberation and all those who have broken their guru's advice. May this negative karma represent every undesirable thing of all living beings. May I experience all the causes and all the suffering results by myself alone; may all other beings be free from all this negative karma and its results."

If you miss your daily meditation commitments, for example, apply thought transformation in a similar way: "May the negative karma of missing my commitments be a substitute for all the problems of all other beings. May I experience this karma on their behalf." Experience every single undesirable thing on behalf of all other living beings.

7

THE HEART ADVICE

❧❧❧❧❧❧❧❧❧❧❧❧❧❧

There is nothing to trust in seeking happiness from outside;
you will only become exhausted with suffering,
which is without satisfaction and without end.

Applying even one technique of Mahayana thought transformation is the best protection. For example, you can apply the verse in *Lama Chöpa:*

> O holy compassionate guru, please grant me blessings to be able to take all the karmic debts, obstacles, and sufferings of other beings, without exception, upon myself and to dedicate my own body and merit to them. Thus, may I lead all beings to bliss.

If you apply even this one verse in any situation, you will be constantly generating bodhicitta, renouncing yourself and cherishing others.

The practice of bodhicitta is your best protection. It gives better protection than spending every life for many hundreds of eons learning to protect yourself with karate. This one realization of bodhicitta is incomparable.

As long as you do not change your own mind, there will always be an enemy to harm you. Even if you own more atomic bombs than there are atoms of this earth, you will not be able to destroy your own delusions or those of others. Even owning enough atomic bombs to fill the whole sky is meaningless. Instead of giving protection, they only give harm. The power of that many atomic bombs is completely insignificant when compared to the power of one good heart. If all the people in this world possessed bodhicitta, we could say goodbye to guns, bombs, armies, and police. Lama Yeshe used to say: "An apple a day keeps the doctor away; a good heart a day keeps the enemy away."

If, instead of putting all its effort into military development, a country were to put all its effort into the development of the mind, of the good heart, it would be in no danger of being invaded by other countries. If the entire energy of everyone in a country were put into developing the good heart, there would be no danger of invasion because of the power of the good heart.

No matter how well developed its military power, a country can never be certain of defeating all its enemies all the time. It does not follow logically that having vast amounts of military personnel and equipment means that a country will definitely win all the time. It is only when the entire emphasis of a country is on development of the mind and the good heart, with everyone accepting responsibility for this, that all success comes. When that emphasis is lost, all other problems follow.

Instead of billions of dollars being spent on defense, the money could be used to provide incredible public services. It could be used to solve the problems of the people of the country and make their lives comfortable.

Take, for example, the Chinese in Tibet. I have not been to China; however, I have been twice to Tibet. Wherever you go in Tibet, it seems that the Chinese have put all their effort into military development. It reminds me of the way a meditator puts every single effort into striving to gain realizations of the graduated path: they eat, drink, and wear clothes in order to train in the lam-rim. They do everything to develop their mind, to achieve enlightenment for the sake of living beings.

Similarly, everywhere you go in Tibet—apart from some luxury hotels built for tourists—there is total concentration on developing military power. Everything is focused on this. The essence of Tibet—its mountains, its beauty—has been destroyed in order to develop military power. The main aim of having this power is to take over others, but in some ways, the happiness of even the Chinese people has been sacrificed. The lives of the Chinese in Tibet are completely concentrated on defeating others, and the services that would bring them comfort and happiness have been neglected.

During my stay in Xining, near the monastery of Kumbum in Amdo, where Lama Tsong Khapa was born, I did not see any happiness at all in the people of that city. All the Chinese I met were unhappy; I did not see a single happy person. While traveling there, looking at the people, I reached the conclusion that there was not even one happy person to be found.

THE BENEFITS OF MAHAYANA THOUGHT TRANSFORMATION

When you are completely determined to practice Mahayana thought transformation, to use suffering and happiness in the Mahayana path, you cherish others and completely sacrifice yourself in order to experience all their sufferings by yourself alone. This is when real happiness starts. When you live your life opposed to the self-cherishing thought, you are happy all the time. No matter what happens, how the conditions of your life change, you are happy.

Training in Mahayana thought transformation makes your mind very soft and light, and you develop a big heart. You are not easily disturbed, and other people feel comfortable in your company. There is happiness and courage in your heart. All the time, day and night, wherever you go, your mind is fully confident, and you live in constant happiness. There are no obstacles to your Dharma practice, and all miserable conditions appear as auspicious. Everything appears as a good sign, and your mind is always content, happy, and peaceful.

In these degenerate times, there is no better armor, no better protection, than the practice of thought transformation. By doing these practices and not allowing yourself to be irritated by problems, you are suddenly released from problems, like an army dropping its weapons. You can even recover unexpectedly from serious illnesses.

When you practice Mahayana thought transformation, no living being or non-living thing can harm you. Even when you are dying, you are able to apply thought transformation and practice tong-len. A person who is able to die with the thought of cherishing others is a compassionate person, a self-supporting person. If you die practicing tong-len with the thought of bodhicitta in your heart, you cannot be reborn in the lower realms. It is impossible. Without any difficulty and with complete joy in your heart, you will naturally be able to experience death for all living beings.

Practicing in this way, you give yourself freedom all the time. This is what is meant by the meditative state of the bodhisattvas known as "all dharmas being pervaded by bliss."

THE HEART ADVICE

The wise, seeing that all happiness and suffering depend upon the mind, seek happiness from their own mind, not from anything external. The mind possesses all the causes of happiness. You can see this in the practice of thought transformation, particularly when you use your sufferings in the path to enlightenment. When you do not think of the benefits of problems—of mixing problems with Mahayana thought transformation and using them in the Mahayana path—but think only of the shortcomings of problems, you label difficulties as problems, and they then appear to you as problems. Therefore, your mind creates your problems.

This is one way of describing how the cause of problems is your own mind, how problems come from your own mind. It is similar when you think of the benefits of problems and use them in the Mahayana path. When you stop the thought of disliking problems and establish the thought of liking them, your problems appear as beneficial, wonderful things.

Any happiness you feel comes from your own mind. From the small pleasure you experience from a cool breeze when you feel hot, all the way to enlightenment, all happiness comes from your own mind, is manufactured by your own inner factory.

All the causes are there within your own mind. Since the thoughts within your mind are the causes of your happiness, seek happiness from your own mind. Seeking happiness from your own mind is the essential point of Dharma, the teachings of Buddha, and practicing thought transformation is the clearest, most skillful way to seek happiness from your own mind.

Your happiness does not depend on anything external—on whether or not someone is angry with you or criticizes you. When someone is angry with you, by looking at them with compassion, you will feel how pitiful they are. By looking at them with loving kindness, from your heart you feel very warmly towards them, seeing them in the aspect of beauty. Using thought transformation, you can see that person as unbelievably precious and kind, as the most precious person in your life, more precious than millions of dollars or mountains of diamonds. Among all living beings, they are the most precious, the most kind.

No matter what harm someone does to you with their body, speech, or mind, even though their intention is to hurt you, by using thought transformation, you see what they are doing as only incredibly beneficial for developing your mind, and this makes you very happy. You can see very clearly that this happiness comes from your own mind; it does not depend on how others behave towards you or what they think of you.

What you think is a problem comes from your own mind; what you think is joyful comes from your own mind. Your happiness does not depend on anything external.

The foolish seek happiness from outside, running around and

keeping themselves busy with that expectation. If you seek happiness from outside yourself, you have no freedom, always have problems, and are never completely satisfied. You are unable to accomplish anything, unable to see things clearly, and unable to judge correctly. There are always so many problems. There are also dangers from enemies and thieves. It is very difficult to have complete satisfaction, complete success.

Jigme Tenpei Nyima gives the following example: No matter how much a crow feeds a baby cuckoo from its own beak, it is impossible for the cuckoo to become a crow. Like this, there is nothing to trust in seeking happiness from outside; you will only become exhausted with suffering, which is without satisfaction and without end.

Jigme Tenpei Nyima then concludes his explanation on using suffering in the path to enlightenment: "This is my heart advice, integrating a hundred different points into one." In other words, many hundreds of pieces of advice on how to practice Dharma have been integrated into this heart advice on how to use suffering in the Mahayana path to enlightenment.

You may have heard nothing new in this teaching. However, if you put this advice into practice, you will see definite and immediate benefit. If you do not try to practice this advice, even though you may have a large library of thought transformation teachings in your mind, your problems will still be there.

Mahayana thought transformation is the most powerful way to transform the problems of life into happiness. As much as possible, try to put this teaching into practice. This is the main thing.

GLOSSARY

Aggregates. The association of body and mind; a person comprises five aggregates: form, feeling, recognition, consciousness, and compositional factors.

Atisha (982–1054). The renowned Indian Buddhist master who came to Tibet to help in the revivial of Buddhism and who established the Kadam tradition. His text, *Lamp of the Path to Enlightenment,* is the basis of the lam-rim.

Bodhicitta. The altruistic aspiration to achieve enlightenment in order to enlighten all living beings.

Bodhisattva. One who possesses bodhicitta.

Buddha (Tib. *sang gye, chom den de*). A fully awakened, or enlightened, being. *See* enlightenment.

Buddhadharma. See Dharma.

Buddha-potential. Refers to the emptiness, or ultimate nature, of the mind. Because of this nature, every sentient being possesses the potential to become fully enlightened, a Buddha.

Cyclic existence. See samsara.

Delusions. The negative, or superstitious, thoughts that are the cause of suffering. The three root delusions are ignorance, anger, and attachment.

Dharma. The teachings of the Buddha.

Disturbing thoughts. See delusions.

Eight freedoms. The eight states from which a perfect human rebirth is free: (1) being born in a hell realm; (2) being born as a hungry ghost; (3) being born as an animal; (4) being born as a barbarian; (5) being born as a long-life god; (6) holding wrong views; (7) being born in a dark age when no Buddha has descended; (8) being born with defective mental or physical faculties.

Eight worldly dharmas. The worldly concerns that generally motivate the actions of ordinary beings: (1) being happy when acquiring something; (2) being unhappy when not acquiring something; (3) wanting to be happy; (4) not wanting to be unhappy; (5) wanting to hear interesting sounds; (6) not wanting to hear uninteresting sounds; (7) wanting praise; (8) not wanting criticism.

Emptiness. The absence, or lack of, true existence. Ultimately, every phenomenon is empty of existing truly, or from its own side, or independently. *See* merely labeled.

Enlightenment. Full awakening; Buddhahood; omniscience; the ultimate goal of Mahayana Buddhist practice, attained when all limitations have been removed from the mind and all positive potential has been realized; a state characterized by unlimited compassion, skill, and wisdom.

Evil-gone realms. See lower realms.

Five degenerations. The degenerations of life span, view, disturbing thoughts, sentient beings, and time.

Five powers. The five are: (1) the power of determination: the force of setting a positive motivation; (2) the power of familiarity: training constantly in the thought of bodhicitta; (3) the power of the white seed: increasing the force of bodhicitta; (4) the power of putting the blame: repudiating self-cherishing, the source of all problems; and (5) the power of aspiration: dedicating one's merit towards the development of bodhicitta.

Four noble truths. The subject of the Buddha's first discourse: true suffering, true cause of suffering, true cessation of suffering, and true path to the cessation of suffering.

Four opponent powers. When purifying negative karma, one applies these four: (1) the power of the basis; (2) the power of regret; (3) the power of the remedy; and (4) the power of making the determination never to commit the action again.

Graduated path to enlightenment (Tibetan: *lam-rim*). Originally outlined in Tibet by Atisha in *Lamp of the Path to Enlightenment*, the graduated path is a step-by-step presentation of the Buddha's teachings.

Geshe. Literally, "virtuous spiritual friend" and a term given to the great Kadampas; now, the doctoral title conferred upon those who have completed extensive studies and examinations at Gelug monastic universities.

Imprints. The seeds, or potentials, left on the mind by positive or negative actions of body, speech, and mind.

Kadampa geshe. A practitioner of the Buddhist tradition that originated in Tibet in the eleventh century with the teachings of Atisha; Kadampa geshes are renowned for their practice of thought transformation.

Karma. The law of cause and effect; the process whereby virtuous actions of body, speech, and mind lead to happiness and non-virtuous ones to suffering.

Kopan. The monastery founded in 1970 by Lama Yeshe and Lama Zopa Rinpoche near Baudhanath, in the Kathmandu valley of Nepal.

Lama (Skt. *guru*). The Tibetan word for guru; literally, "heavy," as in heavy with Dharma knowledge.

Lama Chöpa. Also known as *Guru Puja*; an extensive practice of making prayers, requests, and offerings to the lama.

Lam-rim. *See* graduated path to enlightenment.

Lama Tsong Khapa (1357–1419). The revered teacher and practitioner who founded the Gelug school of Tibetan Buddhism and who was a manifestation of Manjushri, the Buddha of Wisdom.

Lawudo Cave. The cave in the Solu Khumbu region of Nepal where the Lawudo Lama lived and meditated for many years. Lama Zopa Rinpoche is recognized as the reincarnation of the Lawudo Lama.

Liberation. The state of complete liberation from samsara; nirvana; the goal of the practitioner seeking individual liberation.

Lower realms. The three realms of cyclic existence with the greatest suffering: hell realm, realm of the hungry ghosts, and animal realm. *See* samsara.

Mahayana. The Great Vehicle; the path of the bodhisattvas, those seeking enlightenment in order to enlighten all other sentient beings.

Mandala. The symbolic offering to the Buddha of the entire purified universe .

Marpa (1012–1099). A great Tibetan Buddhist translator; a founding figure of the Kagyu order and the root guru of Milarepa.

Merely labeled. Every phenomenon exists relatively as a mere label, merely imputed by the mind. *See* emptiness.

Merit. The positive energy accumulated in the mind as a result of virtuous actions of body, speech, and mind.

Migratory beings. Another term for sentient beings, who migrate from rebirth to rebirth within the six realms of samsara.

Milarepa (1040–1123). The great ascetic yogi and poet who attained enlightenment in one lifetime; a founding figure of the Kagyu order.

Nagarjuna. The great Indian scholar who lived approximately 400 years after Buddha's death; propounder of the Middle

Way, who clarified the ultimate meaning of the Buddha's teachings on emptiness.

Nyingma. The oldest of the four orders of Tibetan Buddhism; the others are Sakya, Kagyu, and Gelug.

Omniscient mind. See enlightenment.

Pabongka Dechen Nyingpo (1871–1941). The influential and powerful lama of the Gelug order, Pabongka Rinpoche was the root guru of His Holiness the Dalai Lama's Senior and Junior Tutors.

Pervasive compounding suffering. The most subtle of the three types of suffering, it refers to the nature of the five aggregates, contaminated by karma and delusion.

Precious human body. The rare human state, qualified by the eight freedoms and the ten richnesses, which is the ideal condition for practicing Dharma and attaining enlightenment.

Purification. The removal, or cleansing, of negative karma and its imprints from the mind.

Refuge. Reliance upon Buddha, Dharma, and Sangha for guidance on the path to enlightenment.

Renunciation. The state of mind of not having the slightest attraction to samsaric perfections for even a second.

Samsara. Cyclic existence; the six realms: the lower realms of the hell beings, hungry ghosts, and animals, and the upper realms of the humans, demi-gods, and gods; the recurring cycle of death and rebirth within one or other of the six realms; also refers to the contaminated aggregates of a sentient being.

Sangha. The third object of refuge; absolute Sangha are those who have directly realized emptiness; relative Sangha are ordained monks and nuns.

Sentient being. Any living being within the six samsaric realms who has not yet reached enlightenment.

Shantideva (685–763). The great Indian scholar and bodhisattva who wrote the *Bodhicaryavatara* (*A Guide to the Bodhisattva's Way of Life*), one of the essential Mahayana texts.

Suffering of change. What is normally regarded as pleasure, which, because of its transitory nature, sooner or later turns into suffering.

Suffering of suffering. The commonly recognized experiences of pain, discomfort, and unhappiness.

Sutra. The exoteric discourses of the Buddha; a scriptural text and the teachings and practices it contains.

Tantra. The esoteric teachings of the Buddha; a scriptural text and the teachings and practices it contains.

Ten richnesses. The ten qualities that characterize a perfect human rebirth: (1) being born as a human being; (2) being born in a Dharma country; (3) being born with sound mental and physical faculties; (4) being free of the five extreme actions; (5) having faith in the Buddha's teachings; (6) being born when a Buddha has descended; (7) when the teachings have been revealed; (8) when the teachings are still alive; (9) when there are still followers of the teachings; and (10) having the necessary conditions to practice Dharma.

Three levels of vows. The *pratimoksha* vows, or vows of individual liberation, the bodhisattva vows, and the tantric vows.

Tong-len (taking and giving). The Mahayana meditation technique of taking upon oneself all the sufferings and causes of sufferings of all sentient beings and of giving to others all one's own merit, possessions, and happiness.

Trijang Rinpoche (1901–1981). The late Junior Tutor of His Holiness the Dalai Lama and root guru of Lama Thubten Yeshe and Lama Thubten Zopa Rinpoche.

Triple Gem. Buddha, Dharma, and Sangha.

True cause of suffering. The second of the four noble truths, it refers to karma and delusion.

True cessation of suffering. The third of the four noble truths, it is the state of liberation from suffering and the true causes of suffering.

True existence. The type of existence that everything appears to possess; in fact, everything is empty of true existence.

True path. The fourth noble truth, it refers to the methods of Dharma practice that lead sentient beings to the true cessation of suffering.

True suffering. The first of the four noble truths, it refers to the fact that all conditioned existence is pervaded by suffering.

Yogi. A highly realized meditator.

SUGGESTED FURTHER READING

Chang, Garma C. C. transl. *The Hundred Thousand Songs of Milarepa*. Vols. 1 & 2. Boulder: Shambhala Publications, 1979.

Chekawa, Geshe. "The Seven-Point Mind Training". In *Liberation in the Palm of Your Hand* by Pabongka Rinpoche. Boston: Wisdom Publications, 1992.

Chodron, Thubten. *Open Heart, Clear Mind.* Ithaca: Snow Lion Publications, 1991.

_____ ed.. *Pearl of Wisdom: Buddhist Prayers and Practices,* Books I and II. Singapore: Amitabha Buddhist Center, 1991.

Dharmaraksita. *The Wheel of Sharp Weapons.* transls. Geshe Dhargyey, et al. Dharamsala: Library of Tibetan Works and Archives, 1976.

Gyatso, Tenzin, the Fourteenth Dalai Lama. *Freedom In Exile.* New York: Harper Row and Collins, 1990.

_____ . *Kindness, Clarity, and Insight.* transl. and ed. Jeffrey Hopkins with Elizabeth Napper. Ithaca: Snow Lion Publications, 1984.

_____. *The Meaning of Life From a Buddhist Perspective.* transl. and ed. Jeffrey Hopkins. Boston: Wisdom Publications, 1992.

_____. *Opening the Eye of New Awareness.* transl. Donald S. Lopez Jr. with Jeffrey Hopkins. Boston: Wisdom Publications, 1985.

Gyatso, Tenzin, the Fourteenth Dalai Lama et al. *Four Essential Buddhist Commentaries.* Dharamsala: Library of Tibetan Works and Archives, 1982.

Gyatso, Tenzin, the Fourteenth Dalai Lama, et al. *MindScience: An East-West Dialogue.* eds. Daniel Goleman and Robert A. F. Thurman. Boston: Wisdom Publications, 1991.

Hopkins, Jeffrey. *The Tantric Distinction.* Boston: Wisdom Publications, 1984.

Kongtrul, Jamgon. *The Great Path of Awakening.* transl. Ken McLeod Boston: Shambhala Publications, 1988.

Landaw, Jonathan and Janet Brooke . *Prince Siddhartha.* Boston: Wisdom Publications, 1984.

Langri Tangpa Dorje Sengge. "The Eight Verses". In *Advice from a Spiritual Friend* by Geshe Rabten and Geshe Ngawang Dhargyey. London: Wisdom Publications, 1984.

Levey, Joel and Michelle. *The Fine Arts of Relaxation, Concentration and Meditation.* Boston: Wisdom Publications, 1991.

McDonald, Kathleen. *How to Meditate.* Boston: Wisdom

Publications, 1984.

Nagarjuna. *The Precious Garland.* transls. Jeffrey Hopkins and Lati Rinpoche. In *The Buddhism of Tibet.* The Wisdom of Tibet Series–1 and 2 by Tenzin Gyatso, the Fourteenth Dalai Lama, et al. London: George Allen and Unwin, 1984.

Pabongka Rinpoche. *Liberation in the Palm of Your Hand.* transl. Michael Richards. Boston: Wisdom Publications, 1991.

Pän-ch'en Lo-zang Ch'ö-kyi Gyäl-tsän. *The Guru Puja.* Transl. Alex Berzin, et al. Dharamsala: Library of Tibetan Works and Archives, 1981.

Rabten, Geshe. *The Essential Nectar.* transl. Martin Willson. Boston: Wisdom Publications, 1984.

_____ and Dhargyey, Geshe Ngawang. *Advice from a Spiritual Friend.* transl. and ed. Brian Beresford. London: Wisdom Publications, 1984.

Shantideva. *A Guide to the Bodhisattva's Way of Life.* Transl. Stephen Batchelor. Dharamsala: Library of Tibetan Works and Archives, 1979.

Thondup Rinpoche, Tulku. *Enlightened Living.* Boston: Shambhala Publications, 1991.

Trijang Dorje Chang and Lamrimpa, Geshe. *The Direct and Unmistaken Method.* comp. and transl. Lama Thubten Zopa Rinpoche. Boston: Wisdom Publications, 1991.

gTsan-smyon Heruka *The Life of Milarepa.* transl. Lobsang

Lhalungpa. London: Granada, 1979.

Tsongkapa. *The Principal Teachings of Buddhism.* Classics of Middle Asia. transl. Geshe Lobsang Tharchin with Michael Roach. New Jersey: Mahayana Sutra and Tantra Press, 1988.

Wangchen, Geshe.Namgyal. *Awakening the Mind of Enlightenment.* Boston: Wisdom Publications, 1987.

Wangyal, Geshe. *The Door of Liberation.* Novato: Lotsawa, 1978.

Yeshe, Lama Thubten. *Introduction to Tantra.* comp. and ed. Jonathan Landaw. Boston: Wisdom Publications, 1987.

_____ and Zopa Rinpoche. *Wisdom Energy.* ed. Jonathan Landaw with Alexander Berzin. Boston: Wisdom Publications, 1976.

Zopa Rinpoche, Lama. *The Door to Satisfaction: The Heart Advice of a Tibetan Buddhist Master.* Boston: Wisdom Publi-cations, 1993.

*W*ISDOM *P*UBLICATIONS

WISDOM is a publisher and distributor of books on Buddhism, Tibet and related East-West themes. Our titles are published in appreciation of Buddhism as a living philosophy and with the special commitment to preserve and transmit important works from all the major Buddhist traditions.

If you would like more information, or a copy of our mail order catalogue, and to keep informed about our future publications, please write or call us:

361 NEWBURY STREET
BOSTON, MASSACHUSETTS 02115
TELEPHONE: (617) 536-3358
FAX: (617) 536-1897

WISDOM is a 501(c)(3) non-profit, charitable organization and a part of the Foundation for the Preservation of the Mahayana Tradition (FPMT).

The Foundation for the Preservation of the Mahayana Tradition

The Foundation for the Preservation of the Mahayana Tradition (FPMT) is an international network of Buddhist centers and activities dedicated to the transmission of Mahayana Buddhism as a practiced and living tradition. The FPMT was founded in 1975 by Lama Thubten Yeshe and Lama Thubten Zopa Rinpoche. It is composed of monasteries, retreat centers, communities, publishing houses and healing centers, all functioning as a means to benefit others. Teachings, such as those presented in *Transforming Problems Into Happiness*, are given at many of the centers.

To receive a complete listing of these centers as well as news about the activities throughout this global network, please write requesting a complimentary copy of the MANDALA journal:

FPMT Central Office
P.O. Box 1778
Soquel, California 95073
Telephone: (408) 476-8435.
Fax: (408) 476-4823.